Taking **EARTH'S** Temperature!

# MELTING GLACIERS, RISING SEAS

Tara Haelle

Rourke
Educational Media

rourkeeducationalmedia.com

# Before & After Reading Activities

## Before Reading:

### Building Academic Vocabulary and Background Knowledge

Before reading a book, it is important to tap into what your child or students already know about the topic. This will help them develop their vocabulary, increase their reading comprehension, and make connections across the curriculum.

1. *Look at the cover of the book. What will this book be about?*
2. *What do you already know about the topic?*
3. *Let's study the Table of Contents. What will you learn about in the book's chapters?*
4. *What would you like to learn about this topic? Do you think you might learn about it from this book? Why or why not?*
5. *Use a reading journal to write about your knowledge of this topic. Record what you already know about the topic and what you hope to learn about the topic.*
6. *Read the book.*
7. *In your reading journal, record what you learned about the topic and your response to the book.*
8. *After reading the book complete the activities below.*

### Content Area Vocabulary

*Read the list. What do these words mean?*

acidification

climate

coral

droughts

ecosystem

fossil fuels

glaciers

greenhouse gases

hurricanes

vectors

## After Reading:

### Comprehension and Extension Activity

After reading the book, work on the following questions with your child or students in order to check their level of reading comprehension and content mastery.

1. *What are some natural and human causes of climate change? (Summarize)*
2. *What would happen if a major predator disappeared from an ecosystem? (Infer)*
3. *What is an example of a way that an animal has adapted to a changing climate? (Asking Questions)*
4. *What is an effect of climate change that could directly affect your community? (Text to Self Connection)*
5. *How can climate change affect people's mental health? (Asking Questions)*

### Extension Activity

Pick an animal you are interested in learning more about. What is the climate in its natural habitat? How is that climate changing or how might it change in the future? How would those changes affect the animal? List at least three ways the animal would need to adapt to survive in the new climate.

# TABLE OF CONTENTS

Climate Affects All Life . . . . . . . . . . . . . . . . . . . . . . . 4
How Humans Affect Climate . . . . . . . . . . . . . . . . 10
Climate Change and Communities . . . . . . . . . 16
Climate Change Impact on Health . . . . . . . . . . 24
Animals and Ecosystems . . . . . . . . . . . . . . . . . . . 32
Oceans Feeling the Heat . . . . . . . . . . . . . . . . . . . 40
Glossary . . . . . . . . . . . . . . . . . . . . . . . . . . . . . . . . . 46
Index . . . . . . . . . . . . . . . . . . . . . . . . . . . . . . . . . . . . 47
Show What You Know . . . . . . . . . . . . . . . . . . . . . . 47
Further Reading . . . . . . . . . . . . . . . . . . . . . . . . . . . 47
About the Author . . . . . . . . . . . . . . . . . . . . . . . . . . 48

# CHAPTER ONE

# CLIMATE AFFECTS ALL LIFE

Think of every English word you know that has to do with snow and ice. If you list them all, it's probably fewer than a dozen. But the Sami people of Lapland, in northern Scandinavia and Russia, have at least 180 words for snow and ice because they live in the Arctic. They are used to a cold, snowy **climate** below freezing much of the year.

An example of how precise Sami words for snow can be: the word *guoldu* means a "cloud of snow, which blows up from the ground when there is a hard frost without very much wind."

A single day of snowfall describes the weather in the Sami people's environment, but weather patterns over time describe their climate. Rainfall, snowfall, temperature, wind patterns, and humidity over time all make up a region's climate.

The Northern Lights seen above Sami homes.

## HUNGRY REINDEER

*Sami culture revolves around reindeer. Their language has about a thousand words that mean reindeer! But increasing Arctic temperatures mean less snow and more rain than in the past. When the rain freezes, reindeer cannot reach lichen, their main food source, because it is frozen over.*

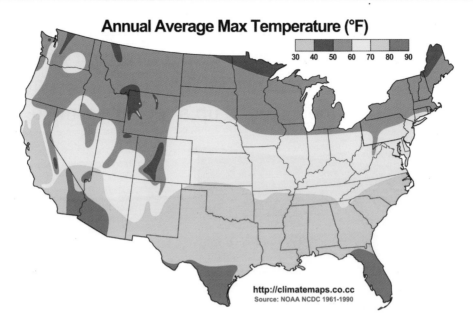

**Annual Average Max Temperature (°F)**

30  40  50  60  70  80  90

http://climatemaps.co.cc
Source: NOAA NCDC 1961-1990

People and animals adapt to the climate where they live. New Yorkers own heavier coats than Texans, but Texans probably have bigger stocks of sunblock. Polar bears have thick fur coats to keep them warm in subzero temperatures, and camels' bodies store huge amounts of water because they live in such dry climates.

Texas summers average 90 to 100 degrees Fahrenheit (32 to 38 degrees Celsius) for several months.

## CITIES UNDER WATER

*By 2100, scientists estimate that 670 U.S. coastal communities will experience regular flooding because of climate change. Major U.S. cities most threatened by sea level rise include Miami, Boston, New York City, Honolulu, New Orleans, San Diego, Los Angeles, and Seattle.*

A region's climate affects nearly every part of animals' and people's lives. People can only grow citrus fruits such as oranges and lemons in warm climates, while most berries grow in cooler climates. Climate also affects health. Texans must worry more about sunburn and heat stroke than Alaskans, and frostbite is a bigger threat to Alaskans.

UNITED STATES CITRUS GROWING REGION

= WARM WEATHER REGION

Winters in northern Alaska can average 6 to 20 degrees Fahrenheit (-14 to -6 degrees Celsius).

Climates change both from natural and human causes, and the world's climate is changing faster now than ever before. Worldwide temperatures have increased 1.8 degrees Fahrenheit (1 degree Celsius) since 1901. That sounds small but has big effects, just as ripples from a stone thrown into water become larger waves expanding outward. An increase of 3.6 degrees Fahrenheit (2 degrees Celsius) would destroy half the Amazon rainforest in South America.

Less rainfall in the Amazon could have disastrous effects on hundreds of species living there.

Eruptions from active volcanoes, such as Mount Bromo in Indonesia, can actually cause the climate to slightly cool because the ash particles reflect sunlight away from Earth.

## NATURAL CYCLES

*Earth naturally experiences cycles of warming and cooling over thousands of years. Volcanic eruptions, ocean currents, rainfall patterns, and the planet's tilt all influence climate too. Astronomical events, such as sun storms or a large meteor hitting Earth, can also cause big changes in the climate.*

The Sami people are used to an average seven months of snow each year, but scientists predict 20 to 30 percent less snowfall where they live by the year 2100.

In the Arctic, where the Sami rely heavily on their environment, temperatures are increasing twice as fast as in the rest of the world. The Sami must adapt quickly to climate change to survive. So must thousands of other communities—and plants and animals—across the world.

# CHAPTER TWO

# HOW HUMANS AFFECT CLIMATE

It's hard to calculate exactly how much climate change has resulted from natural causes and how much humans have caused. Some people think humans have little or no effect on climate. They are often called "climate skeptics." They argue that Earth is in the middle of a normal warming cycle that will later cool off again.

In Spitsbergen, Norway, in the northern Arctic, many glaciers are shrinking instead of growing in autumn. Increased rainfall instead of snow further breaks up the ice.

Air pollution can contribute to chronic disease in people. Hong Kong's poor air quality, for example, leads to higher numbers of hospitalizations for asthma on its worst days.

But nearly all scientists studying climate say Earth is warming much more quickly than in the past—too quickly to be a natural cycle. A report from the U.S. Global Change Research Program in 2017 concluded it is "extremely likely human influence has been the dominant cause of the observed warming since the mid-20th century."

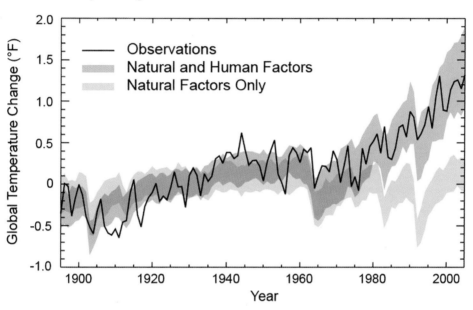

Separating Human and Natural Influences on Climate

## FEEDBACK LOOPS

*As global warming melts more ice in Earth's poles, it heats up the oceans. Warmer water temperatures affect sea life while forcing the ocean to release more heat. Then the released heat melts more ice. This continuing cycle is called a feedback loop. Many such feedback loops contribute to climate change.*

Humans mostly contribute to climate change by producing **greenhouse gases**, including carbon dioxide, methane, and nitrous oxide. These chemicals capture more of the sun's heat in the atmosphere, much as a greenhouse does for plants.

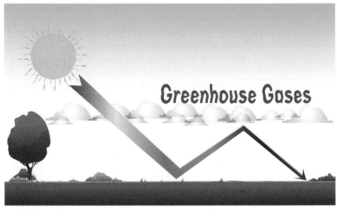

Large oil refineries convert oil into a form humans can use for energy, but the cost of using all that oil is increased heat in the atmosphere.

## THE OVERFLOWING BATHTUB

*Oceans absorb carbon dioxide, and plants use it to make food during photosynthesis. But humans are putting more carbon dioxide into the atmosphere faster than oceans and plants can remove it. The problem is similar to a bathtub that will overflow if water flows in faster than it drains out.*

Natural processes release much more carbon dioxide into the atmosphere than humans, but it's removed in natural cycles. The extra carbon dioxide humans add by burning fossil fuels continues to grow.

When humans burn coal, oil, and natural gas for energy, they release billions of tons of carbon dioxide. The carbon in these **fossil fuels** comes from dead plants and animals decaying over millions of years.

Destroying forests and clearing the land for farming releases even more carbon dioxide into the air. And raising animals for food adds methane from the gas they pass.

As human activities release more greenhouse gases, Earth's atmosphere is heating up. Huge ice sheets and **glaciers**, giant blocks of slowly moving ice, in the North and South Poles are melting and causing sea levels to rise.

Some Antarctic glaciers are thawing in ways that could increase sea levels for centuries.

## PEOPLE WORKING TOGETHER

*If humans are largely contributing to climate change, many think people can work together to slow it down too. Governments across the world are working together to reduce greenhouse gas production, and many militaries and government agencies have developed plans to deal with its effects.*

Increased temperatures are causing other effects throughout the world. Climate scientists study these effects to forecast how the climate will continue changing. Climate skeptics think educated guesses about the future climate are unreliable. But many scientific predictions are already coming true.

Climate change cannot cause a single major weather event, but evidence suggests it might be making flooding from large storms, such as Hurricane Katrina in 2005, worse than usual.

# CHAPTER THREE

# CLIMATE CHANGE AND COMMUNITIES

Scientists expect worldwide warming to cause more severe weather. Temperature affects air pressure, and air pressure changes cause **hurricanes**, tornadoes, and other major storms. Warmer air holds more moisture and causes more water to evaporate, so hotter temperatures change rainfall patterns.

Tornadoes form when warm, moist air near the ground meets cold, dry air higher up. Temperature extremes from climate change may make these storms more common.

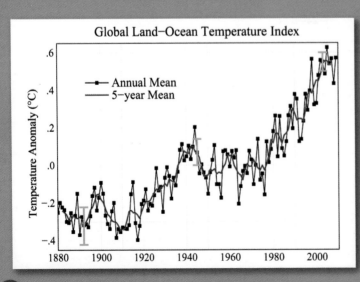

Global Land−Ocean Temperature Index

## HOTTER AND HOTTER

*Humans began keeping temperature records in the 1800s. Since then, 16 of the 17 hottest years happened after 2000, and 2016 was the third year in a row to break the record for the world's hottest year.*

Shifting rainfall can cause flooding or **droughts**, long periods without rain. When drought dries out an area, forest fires become more likely. They also become larger and deadlier.

Countries along the Mediterranean Sea's east coast in 1998 experienced the worst drought in that area for 900 years. A long drought in California led to the largest wildfire in the state's history in 2017. Droughts and wildfires destroy harvests and cause food and water shortages.

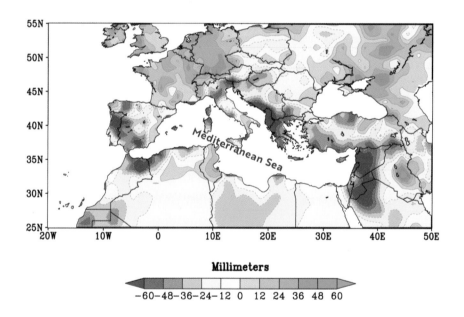

Millimeters

−60 −48 −36 −24 −12 0 12 24 36 48 60

Drought can also affect tourism in places like Lake Tahoe, where boaters had to move their boats during a drought. Less tourism money can hurt local economies.

Periods of extremely high temperatures called heat waves threaten people too. Since 2000, heat waves across Europe, North America, and the Middle East have killed thousands of people.

Like many cities, Chicago is experiencing hot days later in the year than in the past. Seven straight record-breaking days in September 2017 ranged from 91 to 95 degrees Fahrenheit (33 to 35 degrees Celsius).

Hurricane Harvey's rainfall totaled about 24 to 34 trillion gallons of water—about the same amount of water that melts from the West Antarctica Ice Shelf in just one year.

In 2017, the United States had one of its worst hurricane seasons. Hurricane Harvey dumped more rain on Texas than any hurricane in the nation's past. Nearly all of Houston, the nation's fourth-largest city, flooded, wrecking thousands of homes and businesses.

A month later, Hurricane Maria hit Puerto Rico, causing at least 1,000 deaths and leaving many Puerto Ricans without electricity, medicine, and clean water for months.

## WHEN DISASTER STRIKES

*Hurricane Katrina showed how much severe weather can traumatize people. After the Category 5 hurricane slammed into New Orleans in 2005, poorly maintained levees burst, unleashing massive floods throughout the city. Suicide rates more than doubled, and half of survivors developed anxiety or depression. One in six developed Post-Traumatic Stress Disorder (PTSD).*

Many U.S. coastal cities, such as Miami, Florida, have already begun making plans to address the effects of rising sea levels.

Rising sea levels, from melting glaciers, is worsening floods and forcing coastal communities to move inland. Four in 10 people in the world live within 60 miles (96.56 kilometers) of a coast.

An estimated 4 out of 10 people in the U.S. live along the coast, so rising sea levels could affect close to half the population.

Climate skeptics say these fears are exaggerated and humans can adapt to changes. But many people, especially in poorer countries, cannot adapt quickly enough.

## RISING SEAS

*The world's oceans and seas have risen seven to eight inches (17.78 to 20.32 centimeters) since 1900, including three inches (7.62 centimeters) since 1993. Scientists say human activities have played a big role. Sea levels are currently rising faster than any century for at least 2,800 years.*

Stress from lost homes and crops, unsafe drinking water, and severe storms also affects people's mental health. Psychologists have learned the consequences of climate change can increase depression, anxiety, and addiction to drugs and alcohol.

Children and teens may miss more school, have trouble concentrating, get in trouble more often, and get lower grades. Increased family and community violence, homelessness, and crime can all result from climate change's effects.

## SINKING ISLANDS

*Islands that depend on tourism will suffer if fewer tourists visit because of climate change effects. Some tourist destinations, such as the Maldives and Seychelles islands, will disappear completely if seas increase three more feet (.91 meters). The rising ocean has already swallowed up at least eight uninhabited islands in the Pacific.*

# WHAT CAN YOU DO ABOUT CLIMATE CHANGE?

*Climate change is so massive and caused by so many different natural and human factors that it may feel overwhelming or upsetting. One person cannot change the world's climate. But anyone can make small changes in daily life that add up over time. Doing something small each day may also help people who are concerned about climate change.*

## YOU'LL NEED:

- a calendar you can write on
- pen or pencil
- highlighter
- piece of letter or notebook paper
- optional: a computer with Internet access

## DIRECTIONS:

1. If you have Internet access, search for ideas about actions young people can take that offset causes or effects of climate change.

2. Make a list of six to 10 actions you personally can take. Below is a list of possible ideas, though some of these will not apply to everyone.

   - Turn off the lights in rooms you're not in.
   - Close doors immediately and shut your blinds or drapes so heat or cold does not escape.
   - Take short showers and turn off the water while you brush your teeth.
   - Turn off and unplug your computer, electronics, and chargers when not in use.
   - Recycle your cans, bottles, and plastic bags.
   - Use a refillable water bottle instead of disposable ones.

3. Consider your list and pick three or four actions you think you could start tomorrow. Highlight them.

4. For the next week, try to do as many of the highlighted actions as you can each day. Mark on each day of the calendar the number of actions you were able to do.

5. At the end of the week, count how many days you did at least one action and how many total actions you did. Which ones were easiest? Which were harder? Was it harder to do the actions or to remember to do them? Did you have to give anything up to do them? Did any of them take extra time during the day? Do you think you could make any of them permanent habits? Why or why not? How realistic is it to ask other people to do the same thing?

6. Search online again to find actions that require a bit more effort. Some examples are below. How easy or difficult would it be to do these or make them a habit?

   Go the extra mile:

   - Walk or bike if you can (instead of having your parents drive you).
   - Carpool with others or ride the bus for school or after-school activities and social events.
   - Use less paper by not printing things unless you must.
   - Avoid products that use excessive packaging.
   - Reduce how often you eat meat.
   - Plant a tree in your community.

7. If you have a friend or sibling willing to do the activity, compare your results after a week and discuss the questions in step 5. Was their experience different or similar? Does this experience make you feel more optimistic or more pessimistic about climate change? Why? Discussing these questions with other people may help you understand climate change even more.

# CHAPTER FOUR

# CLIMATE CHANGE IMPACT ON HEALTH

Springtime means allergies for many people. In the U.S., 40 to 60 million people suffer from allergies to pollen and molds. Increasing global temperatures are stretching out spring—and allergy seasons. Pollen season increased by two to four weeks between 1995 and 2011. Flowers bloom earlier, and unpredictable weather makes them release more pollen than usual.

Higher levels of carbon dioxide also encourage plants to grow faster and produce more pollen.

Pollen and pollution from burning fossil fuels also trigger asthma symptoms, and asthma rates are climbing. Allergies and asthma are chronic, or long-term, diseases people cannot transmit to others. Climate change can also worsen existing chronic diseases, such as diabetes and chronic lung disease.

Asthma rates have steadily increased since the 1980s. Nearly 9 percent of the U.S. population currently has asthma compared to 7 percent in 2001.

## HEARTBREAKING HEAT

*It's not just lungs suffering from climate change. Hearts are too. The millions of people with heart disease, another chronic illness, have higher risks of heart failure or heart attack. Extreme heat waves and cold snaps strain the heart and can trigger heart attacks. One study found 200 extra heart attacks in the United Kingdom for each 1.8 degrees Fahrenheit (1 degree Celsius) the temperature fell.*

Warming climates also influence rates of infectious diseases, those organisms can transmit to others. Rising temperatures and shifting rainfall patterns are increasing the range of many **vectors**, insects, and other animals that carry disease.

Scientists expect trypanosomiasis, also called African sleeping sickness, to spread from climate change. Tsetse flies carry the parasite that causes the disease.

The *Aedes aegypti* mosquito is known as the yellow fever mosquito, but it also carries dengue fever, chikungunya, and Zika fever.

"Kissing bug," also known as an assassin or vampire bug.

## DEADLY KISSES

*Common Latin American insects called kissing bugs carry the deadly Chagas disease. These bugs "kiss," or bite, people, especially around the mouth as they sleep. While the bug sucks their blood, it transmits Chagas. Increasing temperatures are now pushing kissing bugs—and Chagas disease—further north into the U.S.*

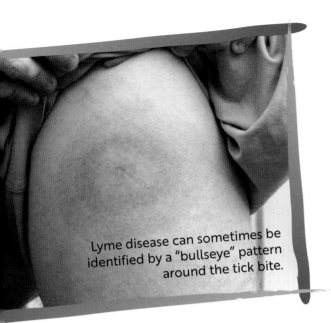

Lyme disease can sometimes be identified by a "bullseye" pattern around the tick bite.

Scientists are studying these effects, such as movements of ticks that carry Lyme disease and Rocky Mountain spotted fever, to see how it might affect the spread of disease. Rising temperatures have complex effects on vector populations.

Just in the United States alone, ticks carry 16 diseases that can infect humans, according to the Centers for Disease Control and Prevention.

For example, tropical diseases carried by mosquitos include Zika, chikungunya, West Nile virus, malaria and dengue fever. These kill millions of people yearly. By expanding habitats of dengue-carrying mosquitos, climate change has helped dengue rates soar 30 times greater during the past 50 years.

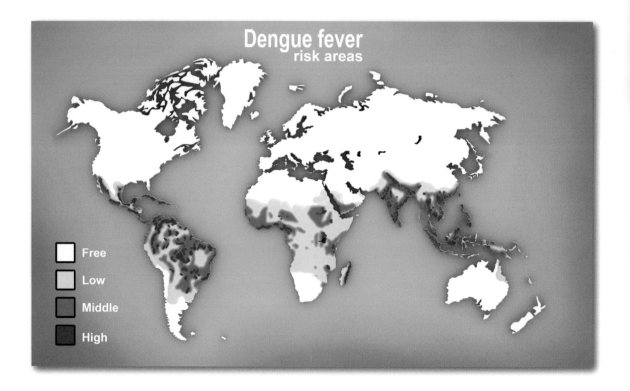

Dengue fever risk areas

Free
Low
Middle
High

Mosquitos cause at least a million human deaths every year — more than the entire population of Austin, the capital city of Texas!

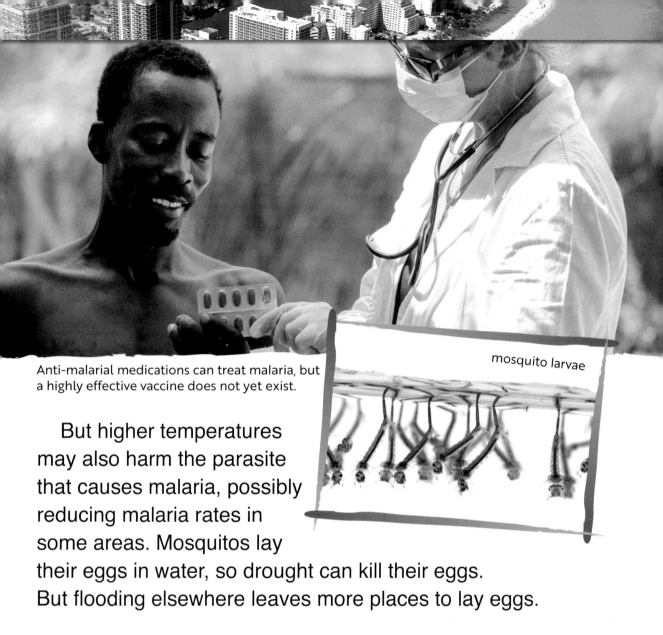

Anti-malarial medications can treat malaria, but a highly effective vaccine does not yet exist.

mosquito larvae

But higher temperatures may also harm the parasite that causes malaria, possibly reducing malaria rates in some areas. Mosquitos lay their eggs in water, so drought can kill their eggs. But flooding elsewhere leaves more places to lay eggs.

## FOOD INSECURITY

*Malnutrition, not getting enough necessary nutrients from food, is another climate change danger. Damaged crops and shifts in growing seasons can shrink farm harvests. A billion people worldwide rely heavily on fish for food, but warming oceans and overfishing are endangering some fish species and making others migrate away.*

Flooding also increases diseases carried in water by microorganisms, such as bacteria, by contaminating water supplies. Bacteria that cause cholera, salmonella, and *E. coli* infections grow faster in warmer water. Severe vomiting and diarrhea from these illnesses can cause death from dehydration, too little water in the body.

Climate scientists take samples to test water for bacteria.

## A SNAIL'S TAIL

*The snails that carry schistosomiasis, a disease caused by a flat worm in the snail's gut, illustrate the complexities of climate change. Higher temperatures cause more snail births—and deaths. Schistosomiasis could increase if the snails move to higher altitudes—or could drop if they stay at sea level.*

The World Health Organization estimates 250,000 more people will die each year between 2030 and 2050 due to problems caused by climate change, such as poor nutrition, disease, and excessive heat.

The World Health Organization works hard to address the spread of diseases such as yellow fever.

World Health Organization meeting room

# CHAPTER FIVE

# ANIMALS AND ECOSYSTEMS

Climate shapes a region's entire **ecosystem**, the local community of plants, animals, and other organisms and how they interact with each other and their environment. Every species in an ecosystem affects the others, from the tiniest bacteria to the largest predators.

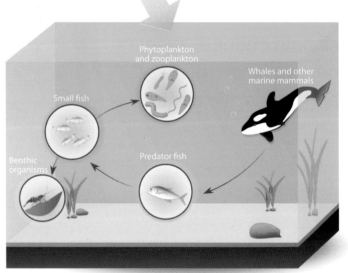

Solar energy

Phytoplankton and zooplankton

Whales and other marine mammals

Small fish

Benthic organisms

Predator fish

Land ecosystems are not usually as diverse as underwater ecosystems, such as this region in Indonesia with more marine species than anywhere else on Earth.

Humpback whales' main food source, krill, eat the algae under sea ice, but melting ice may reduce their numbers—leaving less food for humpbacks.

All creatures' needs remain balanced in a stable ecosystem, but changes that disrupt this balance can threaten its communities.

## SEASONS OUT OF WHACK

*Climate change is changing some seasonal timelines that animals rely on. If migrating birds arrive after flowers bloom or insects migrate earlier than usual, the birds may starve. If animals lay eggs earlier or later than usual, weather conditions may not be best for the incubating eggs.*

The biggest threat to ecosystems from climate change is loss of habitat, the natural home of a plant or animal. Polar bears in the Arctic rely on sea ice to move around, hunt seals for food, and breed. But satellite data from the National Aeronautics and Space Administration (NASA) show Arctic ice melting earlier each spring and forming later each autumn.

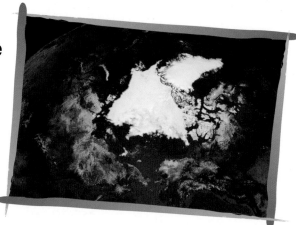

Scientists have found polar bear populations are lower in years with less sea ice, and the bears themselves are thinner because they catch less prey.

## SALMON SURVIVORS

*Since fish are cold-blooded, they cannot regulate their body temperatures. Scientists worried that rising temperatures might kill off the salmon in Norway's Arctic waters. But an experiment raising baby salmon in a laboratory showed they could adapt to higher temperatures than scientists expected.*

Polar bears are great swimmers, but they need sea ice to rest and hunt ringed seals, their major food source.

Scientists have learned that bears are shorter and lighter, and fewer cubs survive, in areas with less sea ice. Banning polar bear hunting in Canada, where most polar bears are, helped increase their numbers. But scientists now expect three of every 10 polar bears will disappear by 2050 because of habitat loss.

Warmer ocean temperatures are also reducing the fish populations Adélie penguins feed on.

On the opposite side of the world, disappearing sea ice is causing similar problems for Adélie penguins, who need ice to raise chicks. Warmer temperatures cause rain instead of snow, and eggs can't survive in puddles. But more than half their habitat will be gone by 2100.

Deforestation threatens squirrel monkeys by making it harder for them to find food.

Even hot, tropical regions are in trouble, such as the Amazon rainforest. Higher temperatures and less rainfall could convert up to half the Amazon into a savanna, grassy plains with few trees, by the end of the century. Thousands of Amazon species could lose their homes.

tree frog

## FROGS IN HOT WATER

*The world's amphibians, animals living on land and in water, are in trouble. Four of 10 amphibian species are near extinction, and more than 30 species have already permanently disappeared. Nearly all frog populations have fallen for two decades because of habitat loss, new predators, changing rainfall patterns, and deadly disease from increasing temperatures.*

Animals face another problem from climate change: disappearing food. When warmer water causes fish to swim deeper or farther away for colder water, penguins have fewer fish to go around.

Humboldt penguin

## WATER FOR ELEPHANTS

*African elephants can tolerate a wide range of temperatures and eat enough plants to always find food. But they drink up to 8 gallons (30.3 liters) of water a day and use it for bathing and play. Droughts can mean danger for elephants, who also have fewer babies when there's less rainfall.*

Puffin parents bring back an average of 10 fish per hunting trip to feed their young.

Snowshoe hares rely on their camouflage to avoid predators such as bobcats.

In North America, puffins cannot find enough fish to feed their young, so chicks are starving. As the snowshoe hare, which turns white in winter, moves farther north to follow the snow, its predators have less food to go around.

# CHAPTER SIX

# OCEANS FEELING THE HEAT

Some of climate change's biggest effects happen below the waves. Corals, ocean animals that live in colonies, form reefs that protect shorelines. Reefs are home to a quarter of all marine species, but many **coral** reefs worldwide are dying.

Coral's beautiful colors come from algae living in it and providing coral food. But environmental stress, such as disease or water changes, causes algae to leave coral, turning it white. Unless algae returns quickly, coral dies.

Dead coral reefs such as this one can't provide fish as much food.

## AUSTRALIA'S BLEACHED REEF

*The Great Barrier Reef, the world's largest coral reef system, stretches over 1,400 miles (2,253 kilometers) along Australia's northeast coast. But it's in trouble. Huge patches of the reef bleached in 1998, 2002, 2016, and 2017. A fifth of its coral died in 2016, and back-to-back bleaching weakens reef recovery.*

Coral can often survive one short round of bleaching but not long, multiple bleachings.

Higher water temperatures are the biggest source of coral bleaching. Just 1.8 to 5.4 degrees Fahrenheit (1 to 3 degrees Celsius) hotter can cause widespread bleaching. When coral dies, reefs fall apart, leaving all those species without a safe home and food. Worldwide bleaching in 1998 killed 16 percent of Earth's coral. In 2005, the warmest temperatures in the Caribbean in 150 years caused bleaching that killed nearly half its coral.

Turneffe Atoll in Belize is one of the most pristine coral reefs in Central American marine waters, but coral bleaching there has occurred more and more often since 1998.

yellow land crab

oysters

A change in ocean chemistry called ocean **acidification** threatens marine life too. Oceans absorb nearly a third of the atmosphere's carbon dioxide, but increasing carbon dioxide levels are making seawater more acidic.

Acidification weakens coral skeletons and the shells of sea urchins, crabs, mollusks, and other shellfish. And these animals play important roles in marine ecosystems.

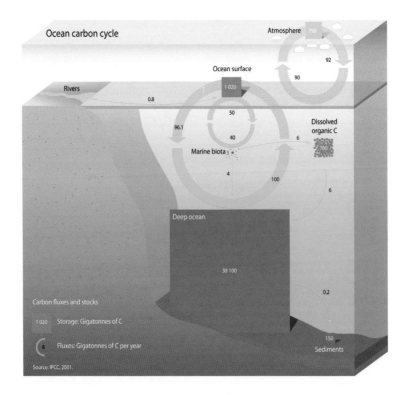

Ocean carbon cycle

Atmosphere 750

92

Ocean surface 90

Rivers

0.8

50

96.1

40

Dissolved organic C

6

700

Marine biota 3

4

100

6

Deep ocean

38 100

0.2

Carbon fluxes and stocks

1 020    Storage: Gigatonnes of C

8    Fluxes: Gigatonnes of C per year

150
Sediments

Source: IPCC, 2001.

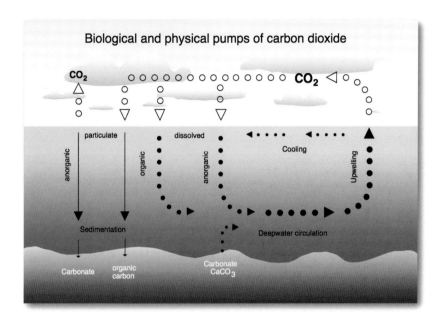

Biological and physical pumps of carbon dioxide

Ocean acidity has increased faster in the past 200 years than in the previous 50 million years. Most marine life cannot adapt quickly enough. Scientists estimate oceanic acidity could double by 2100, the highest levels in 20 million years.

sea nettle jellyfish

## JELLYFISH THRIVING

*Not all creatures are suffering from climate change. Extra carbon dioxide benefits seagrass and algae. Jellyfish populations appear to be increasing since they eat and breed more in warmer water. Unlike most other marine creatures, jellyfish can also survive greater extremes of temperature, acidity, salt levels, and oxygen levels.*

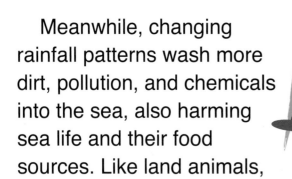

Meanwhile, changing rainfall patterns wash more dirt, pollution, and chemicals into the sea, also harming sea life and their food sources. Like land animals, marine animals will move to survive if they must. But each animal that leaves an ecosystem affects all the others.

Garbage pollutes the seas, harming marine life.

sea turtle in the Florida Keys

## HOT CHICKS, COOL DUDES

*Sea turtles' sex depends on temperature. Warmer eggs (above 84 degrees Fahrenheit (29 degrees Celsius) hatch more females. Cooler eggs hatch mostly males. As growing temperatures lead to more females who can lay eggs, sea turtle populations may grow initially—but entirely female populations cannot reproduce at all.*

# Glossary

**acidification** (uh-SID-if-uh-CAY-shuhn): the process of becoming more acidic

**climate** (KLYE-mit): the weather typical of a place over a long period of time

**coral** (KOR-uhl): found underwater, made up of the skeletons of tiny sea creatures

**droughts** (drouts): long periods without rain that damage crops and cause soil to dry out

**ecosystem** (EE-koh-sis-tuhm): all the living things in a place and their relation to their environment

**fossil fuels** (FAH-suhl FYOO-uhls): coal, oil, or natural gas, formed from the remains of prehistoric plants and animals

**glaciers** (GLAY-shurs): slow-moving masses of ice found in mountain valleys or polar regions

**greenhouse gases** (GREEN-hous gases): gases such as carbon dioxide and methane that contribute to the greenhouse effect

**hurricanes** (HUR-i-kanes): violent storms with heavy rain and high winds

**vectors** (VEK-turs): an organism, typically a biting insect or tick, that transmits a disease or parasite from one animal or plant to another

# Index

carbon dioxide  12, 13, 24, 42, 43

climate skeptics  10, 15, 21

coral(s)  40, 41, 42

crops  22, 29

disease(s)  25, 26, 27, 28, 30,
    31, 37, 40

drought(s)  17, 29, 38

ecosystem(s)  32, 33, 34, 42, 44

flooding  7, 17, 29, 30

glaciers  14, 20

greenhouse gas(es)  12, 14

heat waves  18, 25

rainfall  5, 8, 16, 17, 26, 37, 38, 44

weather  5, 7, 16, 19, 24, 33,

# Show What You Know

1.  What is the difference between weather and climate?

2.  What are two ways humans affect climate worldwide?

3.  Explain one way climate change can cause severe weather.

4.  Explain three ways climate change affects human health.

5.  What are the effects of increasing ocean acidification?

# Further Reading

Sneideman, Joshua, and Twamley, Erin, *Climate Change: Discover How It Impacts Spaceship Earth*, Nomad Press, 2015.

Green, Dan, *Basher Science: Climate Change*, Kingfisher, 2015.

Lawlor, Laurie, *Rachel Carson and Her Book That Changed the World*, Holiday House, 2014.

# About the Author

Tara Haelle spent much of her youth exploring creeks and forests outside and reading books inside. Her adventures grew bigger when she became an adult and began traveling across the world to go on exciting adventures such as swimming with sharks, climbing Mt. Kilimanjaro, sailing the Nile, and exploring the Amazon. She earned a photojournalism degree from the University of Texas at Austin so she could keep learning about the world by interviewing scientists and writing about their work. She currently lives in central Illinois with her husband and two sons. You can learn more about her at her website: www.tarahaelle.net.

© 2019 Rourke Educational Media

www.rourkeeducationalmedia.com

PHOTO CREDITS: www.istock.com, www.shutterstock.com, Cover: glacier © Denis Burdin, miami © Miami2you; Pg4: Vlada PhotoShutterstock.com, titoOnz, Pg05; Ken Phung, Dmitry Chulov. Pg6; APitch, alexkich, Pg7; hlsnow, littleny, kongxinzhu, giorgos245, dianazh. Pg8; adiartana, HotPhotoPie, gustavofrazao, ipopba. Pg9; MeltingGlaciers_P08c, NataGolubnycha, Vadim_Nefedov. Pg10;bushton3, sodar99 Pg11; National Research Council, 2011d. Pg12; amandine45, johnrandallalves, Evening_T, Small_World. Pg13; DmitriyKazitsyn, SteveMcsweeny, TomasSereda. Pg14; Kilav, leonello, NOAA. Pg15; burroblando, joeynick. Pg16; mdesigner125, kulkann, NOAA. Pg17; Eddie Hernandez Photography, SashaBuzko, releon8211. Pg18; LouieBaxter, DragonImages. Pg19; NASA, Citysqwirl, FEMA. Pg20; NASA, byronwmoore, SeanPavonePhoto. Pg21; hongquang09, rmnunes. Pg22; monkeybusinessimages, KatarzynaBialasiewicz. Pg23; Wavebreakmedia, undefined undefined, 9comeback. Pg24; Wavebreakmedia, Rvo233. Pg25; Wojciech Kozielczyk, TRAVEL67. Pg26; auimeesri, NERYX, Meletios Verras. Pg27; Ladislav Kubeš, JerryCallaghan. Pg28; Isarapic, CDC. Pg29; Avatar_023, emer1940, paulprescott72. Pg30; Irina Vodneva, monkeybusinessimages, MarkMirror. Pg31; World Health Organization. Pg32; Designua | Dreamstime.com, Velvetfish. Pg33; Velvetfish, iv-serg. Pg34; NASA, HenriVdl, 3D_generator. Pg35; zanskar, Flinster007. Pg36; alfnqn, Jacynthroode. Pg37; filipefrazao, xeni4ka, engabito. Pg38; joegolby, nicky39. Pg39; CreativeNature_nl, falun. Pg40; Soft_Light, mihtiander, Placebo365. Pg41;FishTales, Velvetfish. Pg42; NDREYGUDKOV, Pg43; Shutterphuma, naturediver, gracethang, Velvetfish. Pg44; WoutervandenBroek, Nigel_Wallace, Pg45; Fine Art Photos, SheraleeS.

Edited by: Keli Sipperley

Produced by Blue Door Education for Rourke Educational Media. Cover and Interior design by: Jennifer Dydyk

Melting Glaciers, Rising Seas / Tara Haelle
(Taking Earth's Temperature)
ISBN 978-1-64156-448-9 (hard cover)
ISBN 978-1-64156-574-5 (soft cover)
ISBN 978-1-64156-692-6 (e-Book)
Library of Congress Control Number: 2018930475

Rourke Educational Media

Printed in the United States of America, North Mankato, Minnesota